Neon Aliens

ATE MY HOMEWORK

AND OTHER POEMS

NICK CANNON

Neon Aliens

ATE MY HOMEWORK

AND OTHER POEMS

SCHOLASTIC INC.

Illustration credits:
Nick Cannon: pp. 12-13, 58-59, 90-91, 124-125
Art Mobb: pp. 22-23, 48-49, 54-55, 64-65, 78-79, 104-105, 114-115, 129
caliFAWNia: pp. 36-37, 50-51, 56-57, 62-63, 70, 96-97, 101, 120-121, 130-131
Captain Kris: pp. 5-6, 14-15, 24-25, 28-29, 40-41, 44-45, 60-61, 75, 80-81, 102-103, 134
MAST: pp. 7, 19, 34-45, 46-47, 68-69, 76-77, 82-83, 88-89, 98-99, 110-113, 122-123
Mike P: pp. 18, 34-35, 38, 84-85, 92-95, 108-109, 117-118
Morf: pp. 16-17, 20-21, 26, 30-33, 42-43, 72, 86, 126-127, 130-133, 135
Queen Andrea: pp. 1-2, 4, 52-53, 66-67, 106-107, 136-137, 143-144; typography pp. 3, 5, 8, 10, 138-142

Cover art by Captain Kris; Cover typography by Queen Andrea
Cover and interior Art Direction by Paul W. Banks
Edited by Samantha Schutz

ISBN 978-0-545-80178-2

10 9 8 7 6 5 4 3 2 1   15 16 17 18 19/0

Printed in the U.S.A.   23
This edition printing, January 2015

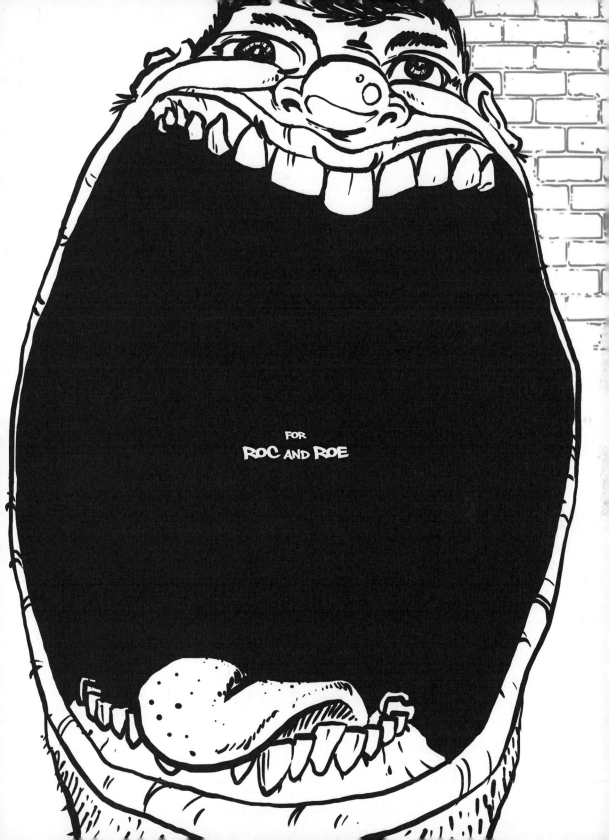

FOR
ROC AND ROE

Thanks for checking out my poetry book, *Neon Aliens Ate My Homework*. I was inspired to write this book as a way to combine the worlds of poetry and hip-hop—two things that have shaped me into the artist that I am today.

A lot of these poems are autobiographical, with a healthy dash of imagination to spice things up! My hope is that you will laugh, think, and say *Ewww* as you read some funny, gross, wacky, and thought-provoking poems.

In writing this book, I wanted to do something unique and pay respect to the elements of hip-hop, so each poem is illustrated by an incredible street artist who has shown his or her work on walls all over the world. There are also four poems that I illustrated myself.

Writing is at the center of everything I do as an artist: music, comedy, and creating stories for television and film. The first important writer in my life was Shel Silverstein. When I was a kid, *A Light in the Attic* was the first book that I read on my own. Seeing how someone could rhyme so skillfully and also be so funny made me fall in love with writing. Seeing his whimsical sketches got me interested in art, too.

Other than Shel, the poets who inspired me when I was a kid were the storytellers of the street: rappers. In my eyes, their stories were no different from the ones that Shel created in his wonderful books—the only difference was that these rappers' poems could be heard over beats that blared out of my boom box.

I wanted to be a part of that movement. I *had* to! When I was eight years old, I got a spiral notebook and wrote my first poem/rap. It was called "Cars." I still remember how it goes: "Lamborghini, Ferrari, Mercedes-Benz. To get one of these you gotta have endz. Talkin' 'bout dollars; in other words, Big Bucks! You can't go riding around in those Farmer Trucks!" From that day on, I could always be found writing in that notebook. I filled it with poems to girls I had crushes on, rhymes, jokes, and witty stories. My raps developed into roasts about fellow students and friends, which would later inspire my music albums and the hip-hop improv-comedy show, *Wild 'N Out,* that I created for MTV.

Doing creative writing—especially writing poetry—is when I felt the calmest and the freest. As a kid, it was my escape from inner-city pitfalls, such as gang violence and other peer pressures. After that, I never went anywhere without my notebook to write and draw in, and I still keep one to this day.

I hope these poems make you want to get out a pen and piece of paper to write or draw your own thoughts, rhymes, and stories.

Nick Cannon

REMEMBERING SHEL

He was a man I never met,
Yet to him I am forever in debt.
He changed my life with just his words.
The utmost respect is what he deserves.
He made me smile in my tough times,
He encouraged me to live life through my rhymes.
He shared his great gift, words like pearls,
And still dispenses joy for boys and girls.
Though he is no longer here,
Through his words you can see him crystal clear.
If you want to meet him, just open a book,
Turn on the light in the attic, and take a look.
Where the sidewalk ends you'll find a giving tree.
Thank you, Shel, for all you've given to me.

NEON ALIENS ATE MY HOMEWORK

Okay, I know this sounds totally berserk,
But last night, neon aliens ate my homework!
They zoomed down right above my home
And zapped me up inside their dome.
These little green guys glowed brightly in the dark.
Their dripping fangs snapped with the force of a shark.
I was scared out of my wits not knowing my fate,
Thinking to myself, *I'm gonna be next on their plate!*
What would satisfy the hunger of these guys?
Would they leave me alone if they heard my cries?
I offered them my notebook and even my backpack.
I feared they could make me disappear with a ZIP ZAP!

The aliens weren't done; they still wanted something to eat,
So I took out my totally finished algebra worksheet.
That did the trick, and they sent me home without warning.
When I got back, it was eight o'clock the next morning.
I ran in the house and cried for my mom.
She hugged me tight and told me to keep calm.
Mom said, "Just tell your teacher the whole story.
She'll understand what happened—don't you worry.
Alien invasions are common in this nation,
And so are kids with fantastic imaginations."

THE GABULOUS GAZZOOR

Good news! Chores are a bore no more!
Just get a Gabulous Gazzoor to clean your floor!
It's fabulous for sure! It will endure your every chore!
From grocery shopping and cutting coupons at the store,
To collecting seashells on messy seashores!
The Gabulous Gazzoor washes windows and doors!
It waits tables, sets plates, and your drink, it will pour!
Takes out the trash in a dash—it soars!
And that's not all—just wait! There's more!
The Gabulous Gazzoor will store your apple cores!
And when you nap, it makes sure you don't snore!
The Gabulous Gazzoor, I'm sure you'll adore!
It never bites or squeaks, nor does it roar!
It's one of a kind, with a special allure!
You should own more than one—how about three or four?
I have a full store—Gabulous Gazzoors galore!
Please, please, please! Just buy one more!

GRAFFITI DREAMS

I sleep wrapped in colors, I can hear the call
Wild styles, tags, murals fill the walls
Fluorescent, pastel, bold, black-and-white
My visions stand out in the darkest of nights
Monsters of creativity haunt my mind
A journey of thought I cannot help but find
Lost in my passion, I spray my heart away
I breathe graffiti and dream of a new day

"Doctor, it's my birthday, and I've got a tummy ache."
He said, "Tell me the problem, and I'll tell you what to take."
"I got heartburn when I ate up all my birthday cake."
"Take off the candles before you eat, for goodness' sake!"

HATERS

Haters like to bully, but I will not waver.

Haters think they're tough, but I'm the one who's braver.

Haters are doubters, and I'm a believer.

Haters are cowards, and I'm an achiever.

One day when I'm older, living my dream,

I'll let that hate melt away, just like ice cream.

SUPER MOM

She can multitask with lightning-fast hands,
And the brightest of lights shines wherever she stands.
She goes to work in the morning, conquers school at night.
She can read minds and knows how to break up a fight.
She's got another set of eyes in the back of her head,
And she perfectly cooks, cleans, and makes up the bed.
Her kisses are magic — there's healing medicine in her lips.
She's soft yet tough, and carries a whole bag of tricks.
She is always ready to answer when duty calls.
She knows when a single pen drops and can hear through walls.
She finds needles in haystacks, is worth her weight in gold.
She is wise beyond her years, yet she never grows old.
When you've got a problem, she's the only one to tell.
She'll come to your rescue if you just call or yell . . .
"Mom!"

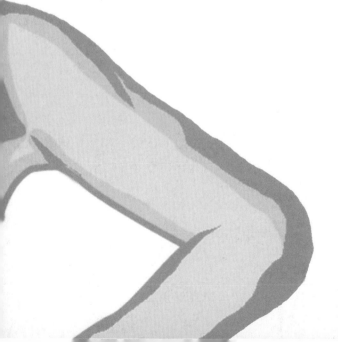

VEGETARIAN FARTS

Vegetarian farts are just the worst.
It's like all those greens have got a curse.
Is it the lack of meat that makes you reek,
Or have the veggies reached their peak?
When that foul odor escapes as a gas,
The smell can clear out an entire class!
So I ask you over and over again,
"Is that stench worth being a vegetarian?"

SUPER MARKET

If you want to go from being a zero
To the most extraordinary hero,
There is a unique place you have to target.
Give the secret knock, you'll meet Mr. Sparkett.
Here you can buy superpowers on sale—
Perfect for mortals looking to never fail!
Utility belts, invisible cloaks,
X-ray vision, supervillain practical jokes,
Powerful mallets, and indestructible suits.
Neon lasers, shiny rocket booster boots,
Smoke bombs, and other disappearing tricks.
And every Sunday, a discount on sidekicks!
Mr. Sparkett has catchphrases and sound effects,
And while he never takes any personal checks,
Mr. Sparkett gives credit whenever it's due—
Here, you'll go from Ordinary Joe to Super You!
But mind control and mystical abilities
Also come with the greatest responsibilities,
So don't get mad if your problems don't disappear,
Because there are no returns taken here!

HOT SAUCE ON ON MY POPCORN

I like hot sauce on my popcorn.

Yeah, I know it's weird!

But not as weird as hot sauce on top of a beaver's beard.

I like hot sauce on my popcorn.

Yeah, I know it's strange!

But not as strange as hot sauce on a handful of change.

I like hot sauce on my popcorn.

Yeah, I know it's funny.

But not as funny as hot sauce on a beehive full of honey.

I like hot sauce on my popcorn.

Yeah, I know it's odd.

But not as odd as hot sauce dripped all over my mom's iPod.

I like hot sauce on my popcorn.

Yeah, I know it's bizarre.

But not as bizarre as hot sauce on a bean-shaped car.

I like hot sauce on my popcorn.

Yeah, I know it's silly.

But really, it's the best thing since hot chili!

THE MOST FANTASTIC, WHIMSICAL, AMAZING STORY

Do you want to hear the most fantastic, whimsical, amazing story?

No?

You're probably right.

It would be rather boring.

DADDY'S SHOES

One day I tried on Daddy's shoes
They were warm and worn with lots of use
Heavy, they dragged with years of weight
His ordered steps revealed by inevitable fate
The path he cleared, the trail he blazed
His feet of bronze and silver tongue controlled the gold he paved
Streets were hard yet he ran for days,
Navigated his way through the worldly maze

An evergreen obstacle to him was a mere stump

The mountain of complication was nothing but a bump

Life was his marathon, and his hurdles were made to jump

Stood on the tips of his toes to overlook any slump

On my imaginary mantel, there I place his pair, so I may never lose

And I can only dream that I could walk a mile in my daddy's shoes

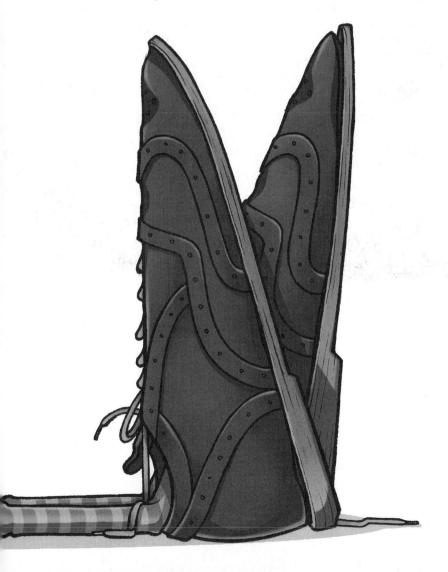

I'm more than smart
I'm sorta like brilliant
I'm more than strong
I'm sorta like resilient
I'm more than fast
I'm sorta like lightning

I'm more than tough
I'm sorta like frightening
I'm more than a worker
I'm the boss-man
I'm more than cool
I'm sorta like awesome

MATEO

Mateo means *a gift from the most high.*
A young warrior, his vision set on the sky.
Mateo, Mateo, with fire in his soul,
He lives with a king's heart, embracing his role.
He's got battle scars, but never lost a fight.
He's young as the day, but as wise as the night.
Mateo, Mateo, our prayers have an answer.
Mateo, Mateo, victorious over cancer.

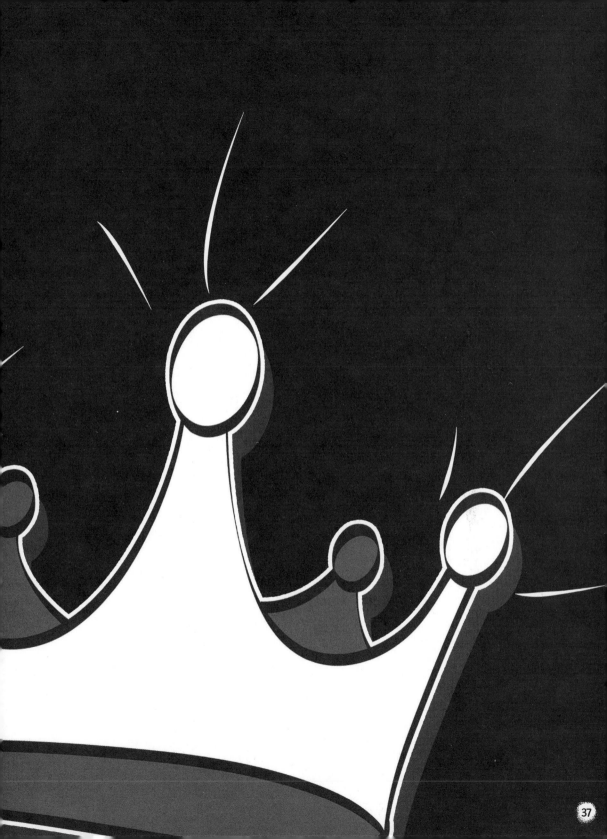

TURN ON THE STRONG

Turn on, turn on!
You know I'm strong.
Hate on me, you know you're wrong.
Turn on, turn on!
You know I'm blessed.
Hate on that, and you'll be stressed.
Turn on, turn on!
You know I'm free.
Hate on this, you can't change me.
Turn on, turn on!
You know I'm fly.
Hate on this poem . . . but why?

PINK LUNCH LADY

The lunch lady wears pink and has purple hair.
She freaks me out with her lingering glare.
Her voice is deep, and her glasses are thick.
Her hands are rough and rigid like a brick.
She serves up Spam, liverwurst, and brussels sprouts.
And she seems amused by all the students' pouts.
It's not that she's creepy and has warts like a toad;
It's that she spits in the food—that's against health code!

POSITIVE VS. NEGATIVE

A negative sees a positive, and it must attack.
The positive can see all that the negative lacks.
The negative jumps into the ring, ready for a fight.
The positive bobs and dodges the negative all night.
The negative swings, wildly determined to win this bout.
The positive sidesteps, and so the negative knocks itself out.

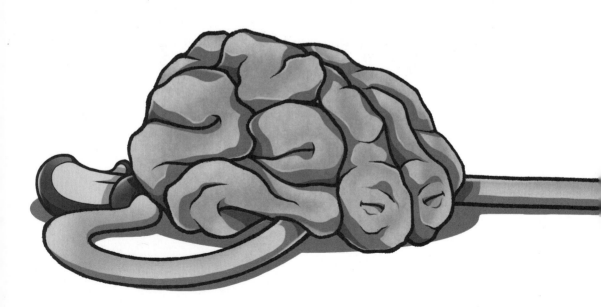

GREAT GRADES

Good grades? Nope. I call them great!
I do well in History because I'm always late.
At Science, I'm a natural-born whiz,
Because I experiment when taking a quiz.
In Swim class, I should have been given a medal,
Because all my grades are below C level.
I guess in Math class, the best finish last,
Because my test had zeros and ended up in the trash.
In Literature, my essay was very, very dramatic.
I received an F . . . I bet it stands for Fantastic.
I'm making it through school with the greatest of ease.
I'm an optimist, so who needs As and Bs?
I guess that's why my teachers say I may never leave!

FUNKY FEET

Oooh-weee!
Do you smell that?
It can't be.
Is it the cat?
Possibly.
Can you tell me
What to think?

This is one
Bad stink!
Time to flee.
This ain't no treat.
Oh, gee . . .
It's your funky feet!

My Mic

Who would I be without my mic, my mic, my mic?
What would I be without my mic, my mic, my mic?
Where would I be without my mic, my mic, my mic?
How could I be without my mic, my mic, my mic?

Mic keeps me out of beef and plenty of fights.
When a brotha's got a grudge, Mic makes it right.
When a crowd won't budge, Mic gets them moving.
Need to tear down the club? Mic gets them grooving.

Who would I be without my mic, my mic, my mic?
What would I be without my mic, my mic, my mic?
Where would I be without my mic, my mic, my mic?
How could I be without my mic, my mic, my mic?

UGLY SWEATER PARTY

It's an Ugly Sweater Party!
Hurry up, you don't wanna be tardy.
It's an Ugly Sweater Ball!
Everyone is welcome—come one, come all!
It's an Ugly Sweater Jam!
Show up warm and fuzzy like a lamb.
It's an Ugly Sweater Bash!
Hope you don't catch a really itchy rash.
It's an Ugly Sweater Shindig!
So get down and dance like a bigwig.

It's an Ugly Sweater Celebration!
Wear the one from Christmas vacation.
It's an Ugly Sweater Fiesta!
Colorful like a court jesta'!
It's an Ugly Sweater Sock Hop!
Wear it inside out with some flip-flops.
It's an Ugly Sweater Rave!
You don't have to behave or even shave.
It's an Ugly Sweater Gala!
Wear the one with a yellow umbrella.
It's an Ugly Sweater Soiree!
My grandma got this one from Norway.
It's an Ugly Sweater Fling!
Finally, I can wear this ugly thing!

THE BABY

My mommy hired a brand-new babysitter
To look after me and, of course, my baby sister.
But there is something strange about this lady, Mister!
Wearing her white fur while inside made us all whisper.
And how she held my sister made her whimper.

SQUISHER

I don't think this job description actually fits her
Because she is very, very big with crazy whiskers.
And now she's actually sitting on top my baby sister!
Could someone please take away the Baby Squisher?

SCHOOL OF HIP-HOP

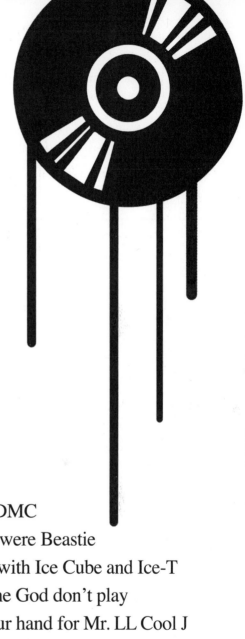

Kool Herc the Founder
Flash the Grandmaster
KRS-One the Professor
Coach Busy Bee and Kool Moe Dee
Instructed on how to battle a word wrestler
Chuck D the Lecturer
While Flav had a love for PE
But my favorite three teachers were RUN DMC
The girls were Salt N Pepa while the Boys were Beastie
After recess we cooled down, cold chillin' with Ice Cube and Ice-T
Eric B. & Rakim taught us work because the God don't play
Todd made the class Hard as Hell, raise your hand for Mr. LL Cool J
Wanted to receive a degree in N.W.A, the curriculum was
    formulated by Dr. Dre
Doug E., Slick Rick, Snoop, Eminem, Outkast, Biggie, 'Pac, Nas, and Jay
Hopefully, one day I can graduate and proudly say Hip-Hop Hooray!

JEWEL IN THE JUNK

My mom says cleanliness is next to godliness.
But let's be honest, how odd is this:
God made dirt, so dirt don't hurt—
Especially if it's a little on your shirt.
I never dust and hate cleaning my room;
I don't know how to vacuum and never use a broom.

On the seventh day He rested, it didn't say He cleaned.
So when I make a mess, don't be so mean.
I'm a great person despite the funk,
So don't throw out a jewel with the junk.

JUST LIKE YOU

High school ciphers were a place to prove I was nice—
Seems like that's what this movement is like.
These industry dudes couldn't move in my Nikes—
Air Maxes, Bo Jacksons, Huaraches.
Before dudes were in skullies rhymin' 'bout Versace,
I was getting chased by bullies. Now it's paparazzi.
They always claimed that I'd never make it.
Once I did, they said I wasn't famous,
Only reason why I'm here is cuz who I hang with.
Got *Talent*? Naw, not me.
I'm just a spectator who loves MCs . . . literally.
Naw, I ain't the best, but me and him shop at the same address.
Same work ethic. Same work stress.
My life is overly dramatic, like a bad actress.
Y'all see me on TV so I musta had more, not less.
But I grew up on WIC and Food Stamps, too,
With dishwashing soap as bubble bath and shampoo.
So you see I, too, am just like you.

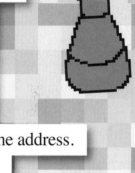

FARTS OR BURPS

Burps are better
Face it
Farts are wetter
Chase it
A fart's stench
Race it
A burp's stench
Can't place it
The moral of the story is basic:
It's better to burp and taste it
Than to fart and waste it

LEND YOUR LIGHT

Lend your light if a friend needs to borrow
Because the hand that you help up today,
May be the one you reach for tomorrow.

Be quick to embrace, and be slow to judge.
For without friends beside you on the way,
The only thing you can hold is a grudge.

BRUSHING MY TIGER'S TEETH

Good grief!
How I hate brushing my tiger's teeth!
I cried, "Tiger, you better open up wide!"
Oh, how his stomach rumbled,
And I just nearly crumbled.

I wish there were another way to keep my tiger plaque-free.
When I put the brush inside his mouth, I think he'll attack me.
I timidly scrub his molars but skip the last three,
Because he's ticklish back there, and he might snap me!
The dentist says I'm doing great, no tooth has been lost.
Only problem is, now I keep forgetting to floss!

See No Monster
Hear No Monster
We No Monster
Fear No Monster
Show No Monster
Give No Monster
Grow No Monster
Live No Monster
No No Monster
Know No Monster

BLESS YOU

Achoo!
Bless You.
Achoo!!
Bless You.
Achoo!!!
Bless You.
Achoo!!!!
Man, put on a coat!!!!!

PUT ON A SMILE

Be who you are, not who the world wants you to be
Love yourself, not the person the world wants to see
Embrace your flaws and turn them into a style
The best kind of fashion is when you put on a smile

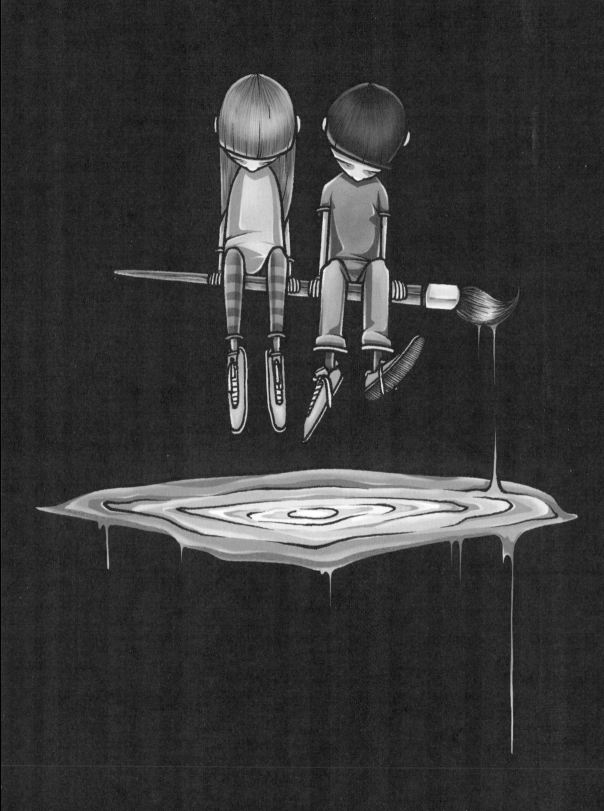

FLUORESCENT ESSENCE

I'm in love with your fluorescent essence
My world turns bright in your presence
Green, purple, pink, blue
I only see you in a neon hue

BACK TO SCHOOL

Parting school is such sweet sorrow
Since there are so many library books to borrow.
Today I read about Mount Kill-o-Man-Jarrow.
I forgot how to spell it . . . I guess I'll go back tomorrow.

Please, please, Mrs. Brenda, no more suspenders!
I like my pants to hang low, but nobody remembers:
I want to be an individual, not an offender.
But to uptight suspenders, I shall never surrender.
Even when it's winter outside, with ice and snow,
I still prefer my pants to hang a little low.
Maybe in summer, I'll pull them up if I'm ready.
But please, no suspenders,
Because they give me a wedgie!

ANIMAL ADVICE

I asked for advice from the meek mice.
They sang, "You'll never go wrong being nice."
I asked for advice from the crafty crocodile.
She said, "Never regret what makes you smile."
I asked for advice from the lordly lion.
He replied, "Make sure your soul is shinin'."
I asked for advice from the rambunctious rabbit.
He squeaked, "Be quick to make kindness your habit."
I asked for advice from the tenacious turtle.
She whispered, "Don't jump an unnecessary hurdle."
Lastly, I asked advice from the burly bear.
He roared, "Believe you can, and you're halfway there!"

ARTHUR'S LITTLE BROTHER

One day not so long ago, Arthur asked his little brother,
"If you have a dollar and ask for another from Mother,
How many dollars would you have in total, little brother?"

"I'd have one dollar!" shouted out Arthur's little brother.
Arthur replied, "You don't know your math, little brother!"
"No," said Arthur's little brother, "*you* don't know Mother!"

PE

Physical education class—
the best place to feel out of place.
Insecure, insufficient, and insignificant.
I've always been the last one to get picked,
And the first one to get picked on.
It's Darwinism in its truest form—
Survival of the fittest.

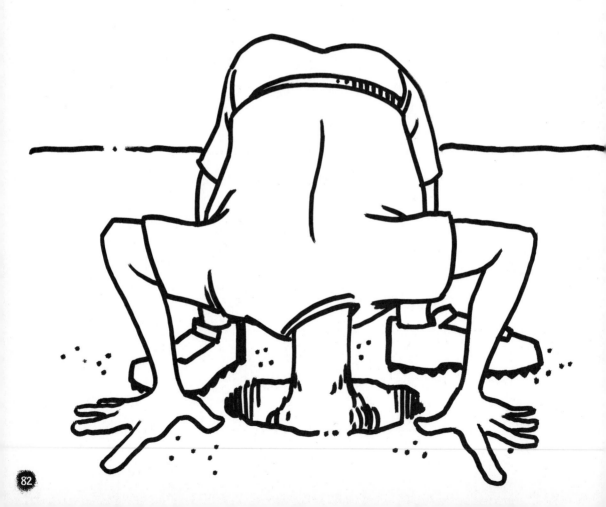

The most vulnerable and revealing environment
In the jungle we call high school.
Go, Lions, Tigers, and Bears!
But in this wild life, I'm like the ostrich—
Prone to keep my head low.
But just when you think it's safe—*SMACK*!
A ball hits you in the face.

TALKIN' JAZZ

Brass
Trumpets
Snares and skins
Bass
Trombones
Flutes and winds
Miles, Ella,
Satchmo, Bird,
Bebop, skat, jazz—
Word!

FLOW IN THE DARK

Fast, I keep spitting
Hitting the switches
I'm just freestyle typing
Writing, my fingers like lightning
So as I sit here in the darkness
My mind is starting to spark
The entire room gets illuminated
My flow is my glow
My screen is the scene

I had candy for breakfast.
I thought it was a good choice.
I had candy for breakfast
'Cause sweets make my mouth moist.
I had candy for breakfast.
I thought Mom wouldn't find out.
I had candy for breakfast.
If Daddy knew, he would shout.
I had candy for breakfast.
It was fun while it lasted.
I had candy for breakfast.
Maybe I should have fasted.
I had candy for breakfast.
It seemed like a good idea.
I had candy for breakfast—
Now I have diarrhea.

BLESSINGS AND LESSONS

If there is pain, there is gain.

There will always be strength after the strain.

Remember these words in the midst of an ache:

When we are bent out of shape, we become harder to break.

MY BARBER WEARS BIFOCALS

My barber wears bifocals on the tip of his nose.

His glasses are so thick, he can't even see his toes.

Can this hairstylist even see? I don't think anybody knows.

This old guy might be better off cutting my hair with his eyes closed.

He asked if I'd like a cut or maybe some cornrows.

So I said, "Just a little off the top, I suppose."

When he was done, I walked out of the shop and almost froze.

I looked at myself in the window, about to pose,

And found my barber had given me a mohawk and four Afros!

When I am lonely is the time that I most need to be by myself
When I look like I'm in great shape is when you should worry about my health
If you see me making a lot of mistakes, believe me I am learning
When you think I'm asleep, know that the candle in my mind is burning

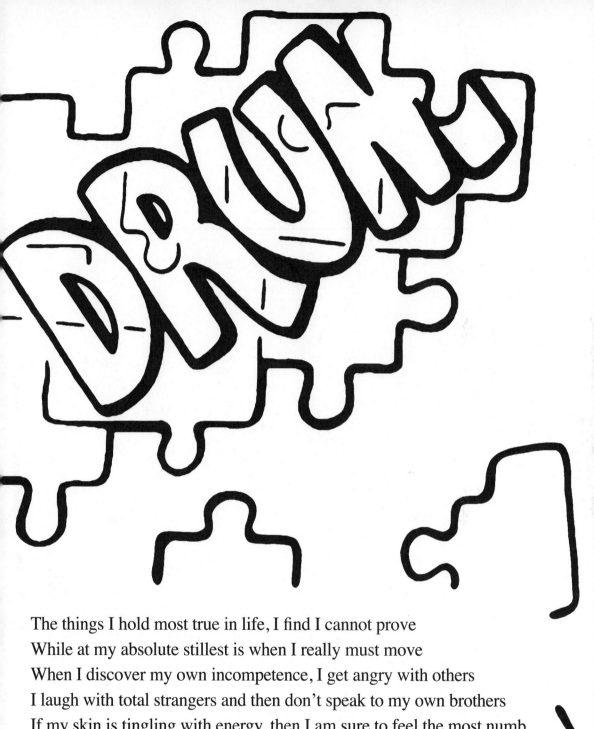

The things I hold most true in life, I find I cannot prove
While at my absolute stillest is when I really must move
When I discover my own incompetence, I get angry with others
I laugh with total strangers and then don't speak to my own brothers
If my skin is tingling with energy, then I am sure to feel the most numb
I cannot seem to escape that I am my own conundrum

SWEET SOPHIA

Sophia is small in stature, but giant in joy.

Her never-ending will, impossible to destroy.

She's strong but delicate, so please handle with care.

Her smile will light a room with a glow so rare.

Sophia, the sweetest child I've ever known,

Searching for a family to call her own.

Her struggle was hard, giving up not an option.

She finally found a loving home through adoption.

THE BUILDING IN ME

Stands tall
Head high
Windows look out
To the sky
Solid steel
Unshakable structure
Smooth surface
Layered with texture
Unshakable foundation
A skyscraper
I light up for my nation

CHURCH LADY'S BOTTOM

The Church Lady's bottom is taking all the space.
The Church Lady's bottom is right up in my face.
The Church Lady's bottom is as big as a boat.
The Church Lady's bottom ate her entire coat.
The Church Lady's bottom has a mind of its own.
The Church Lady's bottom stole my cellular phone.
The Church Lady's bottom just made the nightly news.
The Church Lady's bottom is absolutely huge.
Watch out! The Church Lady's bottom is on the move . . .
Now the Church Lady's bottom is stuck in the pews!

RON ONLINE

Ron Online is quite mean.

He becomes a monster when he turns on his bright screen.

He makes it his mission to be the king of the hurt scene.

He is rude, crude, and the dude is only thirteen.

Insults, rumors, anger, and lies.

Anything disrespectful, Ron Online tries.

He thinks negativity will help him fit in with the guys,

But does he know he's keeping dreams from coming alive?

When he types such pain, another spirit dies.

See, Ron Online does this to cover his own smothered cries.

He is actually a wounded child in his mother's eyes.

When I saw Ron in person, all he could say was, "Brother, I apologize."

LOOKING FOR A SAMARITAN

This gloomy night a fellow walks alone—not a bit of glee.
His thumb sticks out toward the road, a hitchhiker's limb.
He's a stranger in the dark, whistling in a lonely key.
Glaring white headlights blind him with every whim.
He hopes one would stop; a good Samaritan, they would be.
For this to happen, this fellow's chances are quite slim.
For we live in a world where beyond ourselves, we do not see.
In this dim life, we assume his intentions must be grim.
Most people would say, "If I stop, what will happen to me?"
What we should say, "If I don't stop, what will happen to him?"

The game we played as kids:
Mansion
Apartment
Shack
House
Which one would I live in? I want to find out.
Cars?
Kids?
And even my spouse?
Now that I'm grown, I have no doubt,
I won the game of MASH.
Yeah, y'all know what I'm talking about!

Sticky, crunchy, grimy.
Running, hiding, slimy.
Gotta dig deep to find the prize.
Eureka! Gold! Look at the size!

Halitosis is the dirty word of the day.
It means *smells from the mouth that get in the way*.
These conversations will make you dizzy and sway.
I just have one question to ask, if I may:
Why do people with bad breath have so much to say?

JUST TO THROW YOU

It's the worst when people are haters,
And they don't even know you.

Remember, whoever tries to bring you down
Is already below you.

When people talk behind your back,
They're just trying to throw you.

But no matter what they say,
Their actions will always show you.

A CHAMPION NAMED IKIAKA

Ikiaka means *one who holds great strength*
He has true power, yet all thought his life would be short in length
Ikiaka was born outside the angel's fence
Disabilities plagued his core; the weight of his world was dense
But no obstacles would stop this brave young prince
He vowed to leave his inequities, referring to his disease in the past tense
He fought day and night just to stay alive
Doctors were surprised when he was able to survive
He beat the odds like his own sounding drum
Rum pumpa pum Pa rumpa Pump um!

TISSUES

The box is empty—
There used to be plenty.
Now what can I use?
Mom says, "Try a shoe."
Dad says, "Take the rug."
My brother says, "Here's a bug."
My sister says, "Use your shirt."
My grandma says, "Try my skirt."
The mailman says, "Here's a letter."
The weatherman says, "Use my sweater."
The captain says, "Use a hook."
My teacher says, "Get a book."
My coach says, "Use the ball."
My dog says, "Try the wall."
My body says, "Use a chair."
My heart says, "Try the air."
My brain says, "Get a clue."
My nose says, *"Ahh-ahh-choo!"*
Sorry, did that get on you?

We grew up on Weird Concrete

Guess that's why we never feared Concrete

Every color is more vibrant on Revered Concrete

You could even see the beauty in the Blood-Smeared Concrete

We lived far away from the Top-Tiered Concrete

Though we feel ownership because we raised and reared Concrete

Our morals, goals, and, most of all, our word appeared Concrete

Yeah, we keep it real, even on Genetically Engineered Concrete

Though it was hard and rough, we persevered Concrete

When school let out, we cheered Concrete

We learned to love it, when those above it jeered Concrete

We were taught to protect ours when enemies neared Concrete

We came from genuine tough love known as Sincere Concrete

We used our strength to rise above as we cleared Concrete

Sometimes we tried to run away from it, but it never disappeared Concrete

Remember our forefathers and ancestors pioneered Concrete

That's why we should never snicker or sneer Concrete

Because of those who marched and volunteered Concrete

They allow us today to sway and walk cavalier Concrete

Footprints, handprints, date of birth, or that special year Concrete

In the distance, outsiders looked over and peered Concrete

But they will never know how it feels to be speared Concrete

Covered and smothered, immortalized as Frontier Concrete

Mixtures of love and pain we blocked and interfered Concrete

Listen closely to my heart and you can hear Concrete

Trust and believe I live for this Weird Concrete.

Stizinky Wizinky, where have you been?

Stizinky Wizinky, where are your friends?

Stizinky Wizinky, what's your deal?

Stizinky Wizinky, I don't see the appeal.

Stizinky Wizinky, why do you live with this horrible stench?

Stizinky Wizinky, why do you give your own nose a pinch?

Stizinky Wizinky, who started all this rancid funk?

Stizinky Wizinky, who can we call to get rid of your junk?

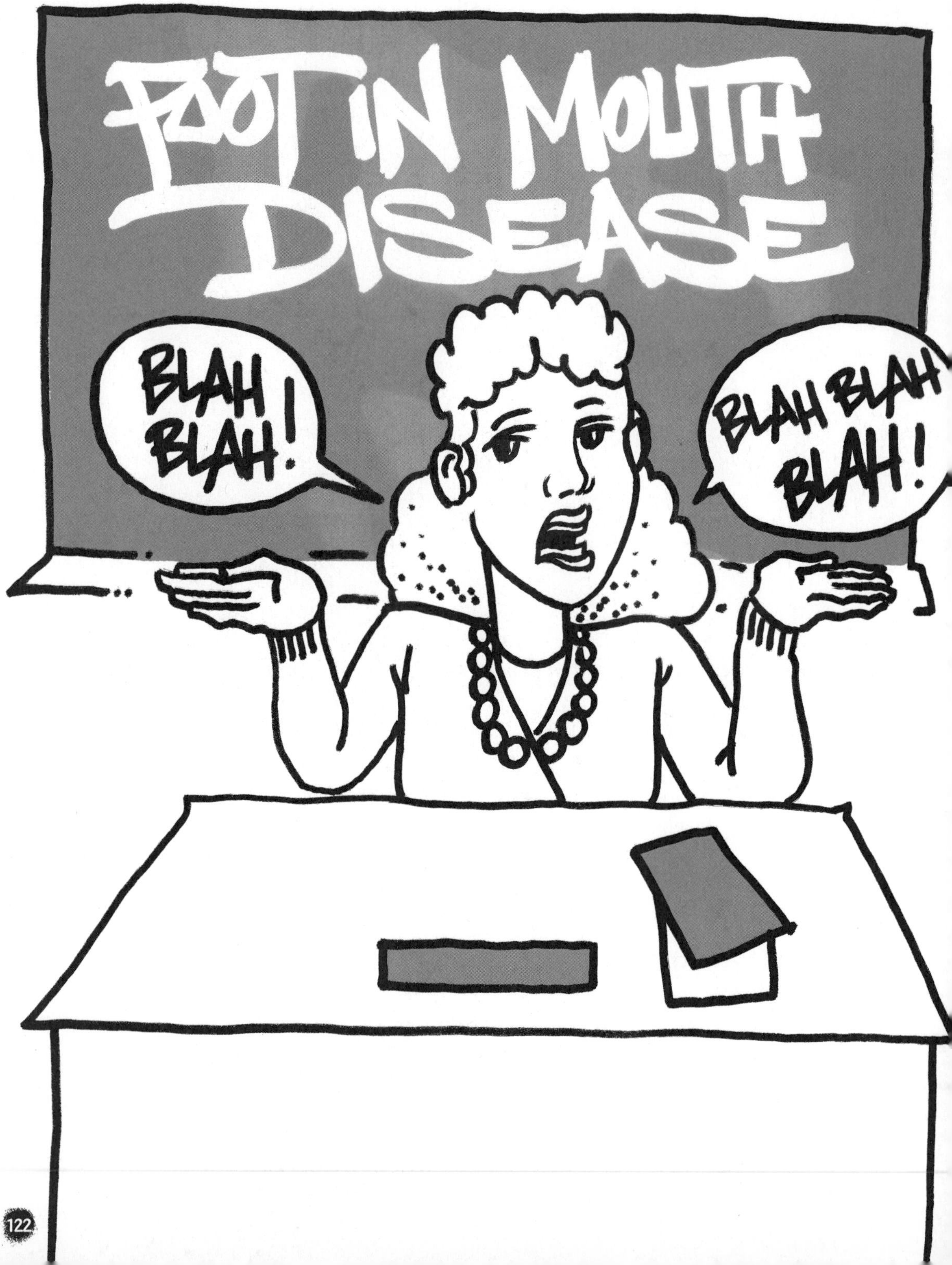
FOOT IN MOUTH DISEASE
BLAH BLAH!
BLAH BLAH BLAH!

My teacher says I have Foot in Mouth Disease.
If this were the truth, then how could I sneeze?
I think what she means
Is sometimes I say the wrong things.
But then, isn't she suffering
From the exact same thing?

GRANDPA ESAU

My Grandpa Esau was quick on the draw
The coolest brotha this side of the maw
Brim hat laid to the side, Cat Daddy was raw
We played Cops and Robbers, and I was the law
Grandpa Esau wore glasses, so he couldn't see as good as we saw
Even though he walked with a cane, he still pushed me on the seesaw
Grandpa Esau loved Grandma
We were all heartbroke when he said, "I'll see y'all…"
We miss you, Grandpa Esau

POLI POLI

Poli Poli
Swahili for "very slowly"
Poli Poli
How the lion prowls solely
Poli Poli
The gazelle glances with one eye only
Poli Poli
African sun rises, its breath is holy

THE ENEMY WITHIN

It's easier to tell the truth than to remember your lies

Never speak with your mouth what you didn't see with your eyes

Walk with purpose and run with the best

Be slow to speak and always keep a mint in your vest

Know that grouchiness and jealousy are useless to feel

Never let emotions guide you, always keep it real

Only follow people who can see what you wish to be

I've met my worst enemy, and he is me

DINOSAUR 3000

The Dinosaur 3000 is new and improved.

This reptile isn't rough and scaly, it's nice and smooth.

The old Brontosaurus was over 75 feet tall,

But this dino makes that Humongousaurus seem small.

His teeth are as big as buildings, his tail as long as six blocks,

And every time he takes a step, the whole city rocks.

His eyes move so quickly you can't tell which direction he'll look next.

His mouth is so big, in one bite he could gobble a whole T. rex!

Both his head and neck flex and spin in 360 degrees,

And he can leap high because of his titanium-spring knees.

Dino 3000 has five sets of wings—all of which he needs.

He's the fastest beast on the planet, with super-duper raptor speed.

He's shiny and chrome, and could walk on water and not get wet.

He can swim deeper than a sub and turn on boosters like a jet!

His giant brain is so powerful he knows what we all think,

And with all these super gizmos and gadgets, he'll never go extinct.

I don't envy the man or beast that comes into this dino's view—

Luckily, it's not until year 3000 that he makes his debut.

SÍ SE PUEDE

Sí se puede

Means "you can do it"

Sí se puede

This is a movement

Sí se puede

Will inspire us all

Sí se puede

Won't let us fall

Sí se puede

It's in our heart

Sí se puede

We just have to start!

LUNCH MONEY

Tommy came home holding his tummy.
Tommy told his mommy he felt crummy.
Tommy was then asked by his mommy,
"Did you swallow your silver dollar, honey?"
And Tommy said, "You said it was *lunch* money!"

HAIKU

A haiku once asked,
"What type of poem am I?"
I really don't know.

I am an artist with words
I think in cursive
I fall asleep with a dream
I wake up with a purpose

ABOUT NICK CANNON

NICK CANNON is a multifaceted artist: film star, comedian, TV and radio host, musician, writer, director, and philanthropist. *People* magazine called this San Diego, California, native one of the top ten most successful young people in Hollywood.

At the age of eight, Cannon began writing poetry and songs, and performing them for friends and family. Through what Cannon recalls as "a lot of trial and failure," he recorded his first song at home on his boom box.

At the age of eleven, Cannon started doing stand-up comedy, and by seventeen, he was performing at world-renowned comedy venues. That same year, he got his biggest break. He became a cast member on Nickelodeon's sketch-comedy series *All That*. Cannon also wrote for the show, making him the youngest staff writer in television history. Cannon's comedy experience culminated in the creation of *The Nick Cannon Show*, which earned him the first of many Kids' Choice Awards—an award show that he later hosted several times.

More recently, Cannon has released several music albums and is the creator, producer, and host of MTV's *Nick Cannon Presents: Wild 'N Out*, an improv-comedy show with musical performances. However, he is perhaps best known as the energetic host of *America's Got Talent*. When Cannon is not in front of the camera or a live audience, he is spending time with his twins, Moroccan (Roc) and Monroe (Roe).

ART MOBB

(aka Michael Farhat) was born in India, and now lives in Los Angeles, California.

English was his second language, and as a child, he found it easier to communicate through his drawings. And he's still expressing himself through art today. "Being an artist gives you an incredible exposure to the world and many life experiences. These help broaden your imagination—which is your most valuable tool."

His favorite children's books are the Babar the Elephant series by Jean de Brunhoff, and The Adventures of Tintin series by Hergé.

CALIFAWNIA

(aka Fawn Arthur) grew up in Ohio, and now lives in Los Angeles, California.

caliFAWNia has always used her creativity as a way to express herself. "As a child I would design doll clothes with my mom, and when I got older she would turn my sketches into outfits for me."

caliFAWNia feels lucky that her art has allowed her to travel the world. Paris, France, is by far her favorite city.

CAPTAIN KRIS

(aka Kristian Douglas) is originally from New Zealand, and now lives in London, England.

He is an imaginative illustrator and street artist who is heavily influenced by comics and cartoons. "From a very young age I have been obsessed with comics and superheroes—something which has translated into the work I am producing now. It even inspired my pseudonym, 'Captain Kris.'"

His favorite children's books are the Hairy Maclary series by Lynley Dodd, and *Dogger* by Shirley Hughes.

MAST

is a "doodler and graffiti sprayer" living in Brooklyn, New York.

"I've always been fascinated by letters, color, and characters—so it's easy to see why graffiti art appealed to me at such a young age." MAST loved that there was always a sense of discovery as he traveled around New York City. Each time he turned a corner, there would be new cartoon characters next to brightly colored, bold bubble letters.

MIKE P

is a New York City-based artist. He grew up drawing as a kid and became interested in graffiti during his teenage years.

Mike has used his artistic talents to add uplifting, colorful pieces to some of the biggest slums in Africa. Today, Mike P is a full-time freelance artist working with galleries and clothing companies. His art can be found in one form or another throughout New York City, as well as many places around the world.

MORF

(aka Jack Fish) is an illustrator and street artist living in Brighton, England.

"I have always drawn and created things in my imagination for as far back as I can remember. Visiting museums and galleries as a child really inspired me."

His favorite children's book is *Wind in the Willows* by Kenneth Grahame. The storyline and characters captured his imagination and fueled him to create his own fantasy worlds.

QUEEN ANDREA

(aka Andrea von Bujdoss) lives in New York City and works as a fine artist, illustrator, graffiti artist, and graphic designer.

Queen Andrea's style was initially influenced by the urban landscape of Manhattan, but she loves getting inspiration from other parts of the world, too. She traveled recently to exotic Tahiti, where she said it was "truly amazing and dreamlike to paint walls and highways in a tropical paradise."

Queen Andrea's favorite children's books are by Dr. Seuss. She adores his wit, wacky humor, and whimsical illustrations.